LOVE LETTERS
OF
GREAT MEN

Vol. 1

Published by SoHo Books
ISBN 978-1440496028
Printed in the USA

Cover Design: Copyright 2010 by Soho Books

LOVE LETTERS OF GREAT MEN

My angel, my all, my very self - only a few words today and at that with your pencil - not till tomorrow will my lodgings be definitely determined upon - what a useless waste of time. Why this deep sorrow where necessity speaks - can our love endure except through sacrifices - except through not demanding everything - can you change it that you are not wholly mine, I not wholly thine?

Oh, God! look out into the beauties of nature and comfort yourself with that which must be -- love demands everything and that very justly - that it is with me so far as you are concerned, and you with me. If we were wholly united you would feel the pain of it as little as I!

Now a quick change to things internal from things external. We shall surely see each other; moreover, I cannot communicate to you the observations I have made during the last few days touching my own life - if our hearts were always close together I would make none of the kind. My heart is full of many things to say to you - Ah! - there are moments when I feel that speech is nothing after all - cheer up - remain my true, only treasure, my all as I am yours; the gods must send us the rest that which shall be best for us.

Your faithful,
Ludwig

Ludwig van Beethoven (1770-1827)
July 6, 1806

Eight days have passed since I parted from f.f., and already it is as though I had been eight years away from her, although I can avow that not one hour has passed without her memory which has become such a close companion to my thoughts that now more than ever is it the food and sustenance of my soul; and if it should endure like this a few days more, as seems it must, I truly believe it will in every way have assumed the office of my soul, and I shall then live and thrive on the memory of her as do other men upon their souls, and I shall have no life but in this single thought.

Let the God who so decrees do as he will, so long as in exchange I may have as much a part of her as shall suffice to prove the gospel of our affinity is founded on true prophecy. Often I find myself recalling, and with what ease, certain words spoken to me, some on the balcony with the moon as witness, others at that window I shall always look upon so gladly, with all the many endearing and gracious acts I have seen my gentle lady perform--for all are dancing about my heart with a tenderness so wondrous that they inflame me with a strong desire to beg her to test the quality of my love.

For I shall never rest content until I am certain she knows what she is able to enact in me and how great and strong is the fire that her great worth has kindled in my breast. The flame of true love is a mighty force, and most of all when two equally matched wills in two exalted minds contend to see which loves the most, each striving to give yet more vital proof...

It would be the greatest delight for me to see just two lines in f.f.'s hand, yet I dare not ask so much. May your Ladyship beseech her to perform whatever you feel is best for me. With my heart I kiss your Ladyship's hand, since I cannot with my lips.

Pietro Bembo (1470-1547)
Venice October 18, 1503

I wake filled with thoughts of you. Your portrait and the intoxicating evening which we spent yesterday have left my senses in turmoil. Sweet, incomparable Josephine, what a strange effect you have on my heart!

Are you angry? Do I see you looking sad? Are you worried?

My soul aches with sorrow, and there can be no rest for you lover; but is there still more in store for me when, yielding to the profound feelings which overwhelm me, I draw from your lips, from your heart a love which consumes me with fire?

Ah! it was last night that I fully realized how false an image of you your portrait gives!

You are leaving at noon; I shall see you in three hours.

Until then, mio dolce amor, a thousand kisses; but give me none in return, for they set my blood on fire.

Napolean Bonaparte (1763-1821)
Paris, December 1795

To Josephine,

I love you no longer; on the contrary, I detest you. you are a wretch, truly perverse, truly stupid, a real Cinderella.

You never write to me at all, you do not love your husband; you know the pleasure that your letters give him yet you cannot even manage to write him half a dozen lines, dashed off in a moment! What then do you do all day, Madame?

What business is so vital that it robs you of the time to write to your faithful lover?

What attachment can be stifling and pushing aside the love, the tender and constant love which you promised him?

Who can this wonderful new lover be who takes up your every moment, rules your days and prevents you from devoting your attention to your husband?

Beware, Josephine; one fine night the doors will be broken down and there I shall be. In truth, I am worried, my love, to have no news from you; write me a four page letter instantly made up from those delightful words which fill my heart with emotion and joy.

I hope to hold you in my arms before long, when I shall lavish upon you a million kisses, burning as the equatorial sun.

Napolean Bonaparte (1763-1821)
Paris, 1797

I have a thousand images of you in an hour; all different and all coming back to the same...

And we love. And we've got the most amazing secrets and understandings.

Noel, whom I love, who is so beautiful and wonderful. I think of you eating omlette on the ground.

I think of you once against a sky line: and on the hill that Sunday morning.

And that night was wonderfullest of all. The light and the shadow and quietness and the rain and the wood. And you. You are so beautiful and wonderful that I daren't write to you... And kinder than God.

Your arms and lips and hair and shoulders and voice - you.

Rupert Brooke
October 2, 1911

To Elizabeth Barrett Browning:

...would I, if I could, supplant one of any of the affections that I know to have taken root in you - that great and solemn one, for instance.

I feel that if I could get myself remade, as if turned to gold, I WOULD not even then desire to become more than the mere setting to that diamond you must always wear.

The regard and esteem you now give me, in this letter, and which I press to my heart and bow my head upon, is all I can take and all too embarrassing, using all my gratitude.

Robert Browning (1812-1889)

Do you know, when you have told me to think of you, I have been feeling ashamed of thinking of you so much, of thinking of only you - which is too much, perhaps.

Shall I tell you?

It seems to me, to myself, that no man was ever before to any woman what you are to me - the fulness must be in proportion, you know, to the vacancy... and only I know what was behind - the long wilderness without the blossoming rose... and the capacity for happiness, like a black gaping hole, before this silver flooding.

Is it wonderful that I should stand as in a dream, and disbelieve - not you - but my own fate?

Was ever any one taken suddenly from a lampless dungeon and placed upon the pinnacle of a mountain, without the head turning round and the heart turning faint, as mine do?

And you love me more, you say? Shall I thank you or God?

Both, - indeed - and there is no possible return from me to either of you! I thank you as the unworthy may... and as we all thank God. How shall I ever prove what my heart is to you?

How will you ever see it as I feel it? I ask myself in vain. Have so much faith in me, my only beloved, as to use me simply for your own advantage and happiness, and to your own ends without a thought of any others - that is all I could ask you without any disquiet as to the granting of it.

May God bless you!

Your B.A.

Robert Browning (1812-1889)
January 10, 1846

And when I have reasoned it all out, and set metes and bounds for your love that it may not pass, lo, a letter from Clara, and in one sweet, ardent, pure, Edenic page, her love overrides my boudaries as the sea sweeps over rocks and sands alike, crushes my barriers into dust out of which they were builded, over whelms me with its beauty, bewilders me with its sweetness, charms me with its purity, and loses me in its great shoreless immensity.

Robert Burdette
April 25, 1898

My dearest Caroline,

If tears, which you saw & know I am not apt to shed, if the agitation in which I parted from you, agitation which you must have perceived through the whole of this most nervous nervous affair, did not commence till the moment of leaving you approached, if all that I have said & done, & am still but too ready to say & do, have not sufficiently proved what my real feelings are & must be ever towards you, my love, I have no other proof to offer.

God knows I wish you happy, & when I quit you, or rather when you from a sense of duty to your husband & mother quit me, you shall acknowledge the truth of what I again promise & vow, that no other in word or deed shall ever hold the place in my affection which is & shall be most sacred to you, till I am nothing.

I never knew till that moment, the madness of - my dearest & most beloved friend - I cannot express myself - this is no time for words - but I shall have a pride, a melancholy pleasure, in suffering what you yourself can hardly conceive - for you don not know me. - I am now about to go out with a heavy heart, because - my appearing this Evening will stop any absurd story which the events of today might give rise to - do you think now that I am cold &

stern, & artful - will even others think so, will your mother even - that mother to whom we must indeed sacrifice much, more much more on my part, than she shall ever know or can imagine.

"Promises not to love you" ah Caroline it is past promising - but shall attribute all concessions to the proper motive - & never cease to feel all that you have already witnessed - & more than can ever be known but to my own heart - perhaps to yours.

May God protect forgive & bless you - ever & even more than ever.

yr. most attached

BYRON

P.S. These taunts which have driven you to this - my dearest Caroline - were it not for your mother & the kindness of all your connections, is there anything on earth or heaven would have made me so happy as to have made you mine long ago? & not less now than then, but more than ever at this time - you know I would with pleasure give up all here & all beyond the grave for you & in refraining from this - must my motives be misunderstood ?

I care not who knows this - what use is made of it - it is you & to you only that they owe yourself, I was and am yours, freely & most entirely, to obey, to honour, love & fly with you when, where, & how you yourself might & may determine.

Lord Byron (1788-1824)

August 1812

LOVE LETTERS OF GREAT MEN

My Heart -

We are thus far separated - but after all one mile is as bad as a thousand - which is a great consolation to one who must travel six hundred before he meets you again. If it will give you any satisfaction - I am as comfortless as a pilgrim with peas in his shoes - and as cold as Charity - Chastity or any other Virtue.

Lord Byron (1788-1824)
November 16, 1814

My dearest Teresa,

I have read this book in your garden; my love, you were absent, or else I could not have read it. It is a favourite book of yours, and the writer was a friend of mine.

You will not understand these English words, and others will not understand them, which is the reason I have not scrawled them in Italian. But you will recognize the handwriting of him who passionately loved you, and you will divine that, over a book which was yours, he could only think of love.

In that word, beautiful in all languages, but most so in yours - Amor mio - is comprised my existence here and hereafter.

I feel I exist here, and I feel I shall exist hereafter, - to what purpose you will decide; my destiny rests with you, and you are a woman, eighteen years of age, and two out of a convent. I love you, and you love me, - at least, you say so, and act as if you did so, which last is a great consolation in all events.

But I more than love you, and cannot cease to love you.

Think of me, sometimes, when the Alps and ocean divide us, - but they never will, unless you wish it.

George Gordon, Lord Byron (1788-1824)
25 August, 1819

I cannot keep myself from writing any longer to you dearest, although I have not had any answer to either of my two letters.

I suppose your mother does not allow you to write to me. Perhaps you have not got either of my letters...

I am so dreadfully afraid that perhaps you may think I am forgetting you.

I can assure you dearest Jeannette you have not been out of my thoughts hardly for one minute since I left you Monday.

I have written to my father everything, how much I love you how much I long & pray & how much I would sacrifice if it were necessary to be married to you and to live ever after with you.

I shall not get an answer till Monday & whichever way it lies I shall go to Cowes soon after & tell your mother everything.

I am afraid she does not like me very much from what I have heard. I would do anything she wished if she only would not oppose us.

Dearest if you are as fond of me as I am of you... nothing human could keep us long apart.

This last week has seemed an eternity to me.

Oh, I would give my soul for another of those days we had together not long ago...

Oh if I could only get one line from you to reassure me, but I dare not ask you to do anything that your mother would disapprove of or has perhaps forbidden you to do...

Sometimes I doubt so I cannot help it whether you really like me as you said at Cowes you did. If you do I cannot fear for the future tho' difficulties may lie in our way only to be surmounted by patience.

Goodbye dearest Jeannette. My first and only love...

Believe me ever to be

Yrs devotedly and lovingly,

Randolf S. Churchill

Lord Randolph (Henry Spencer) Churchill (1849-95)
August 1873

My darling Clemmie,

In your letter from Madras you wrote some words very dear to me, about my having enriched your life. I cannot tell you what pleasure this gave me, because I always feel so overwhelmingly in your debt, if there can be accounts in love....

What it has been to me to live all these years in your heart and companionship no phrases can convey.

Time passes swiftly, but is it not joyous to see how great and growing is the treasure we have gathered together, amid the storms and stresses of so many eventful and to millions tragic and terrible years?

Your loving husband

Winston Churchill

January 23, 1935

Out of the depths of my happy heart wells a great tide of love and prayer for this priceless treasure that is confided to my life-long keeping.

You cannot see its intangible waves as they flow towards you, darling, but in these lines you will hear, as it were, the distant beating of the surf.

Mark Twain
May 12, 1869

I received your letter my ever dearest Maria, this morning. You know my anxious disposition too well not be aware how much I feel at this time.

At the distance we are from each other every fear will obtrude itself on my mind. Let me hope that you are not really worse than your kindness, your affection, for me make you say... I think... that no more molestation will arise to the recovery of your health, which I pray for beyond every other blessing under heaven.

Let us... think only of the blessings that providence may yet have in store for us and that we may yet possess. I am happy in love -- an affection exceeding a thousand times my deserts, which has continued so many years, and is yet undiminished... Never will I marry in this world if I marry not you.

Truly can I say that for the seven years since I avowed my love for you, I have... foregone all company, and the society of all females (except my own relations) for your sake.

I am still ready to make my sacrifice for you... I will submit to any thing you may command me -- but cease to respect, to love and adore you I never can or will.

I must still think that we should have married long ago -- we should have had many troubles -- but we have yet had no joys, and we could not have starved...

Your FRIENDS have never been without a hope of parting us and see what that has cost us both -- but no more.

Believe me, my beloved & ever dearest Maria,

most faithfully

yours, John

John Constable (1776-1837)
East Bergholt. February 27, 1816

Don't write too legibly or intelligibly as I have no occupation so pleasant as pondering for hours over your hieroglyphics, and for hours more trying to interpret your dark sayings.

A clearly written simply expressed letter is too like the lightening.

Cuff Cooper
June 9, 1914

Darling, my darling.

One line in haste to tell you that I love you more today than ever in my life before, that I never see beauty without thinking of you or scent happiness without thinking of you.

You have fulfilled all my ambition, realized all my hopes, made all my dreams come true.

You have set a crown of roses on my youth and fortified me against the disaster of our days.

Your courageous gaiety has inspired me with joy. Your tender faithfulness has been a rock of security and comfort. I have felt for you all kinds of love at once.

I have asked much of you and you have never failed me. You have intensified all colours, heightened all beauty, deepened all delight.

I love you more than life, my beauty, my wonder.

Cuff Cooper
August 20, 1918

For my beloved Wife Elizabeth Cromwell, at the Cockpit:

My Dearest,

I have not leisure to write much, but I could chide thee that in many of thy letters thou writest to me, that I should not be unmindful of thee and thy little ones.

Truly, if I love thee not too well, I think I err not on the other hand much. Thou art dearer to me than any creature; let that suffice.

The Lord hath showed us an exceeding mercy: who can tell how great it is. My weak faith hath been upheld. I have been in my inward man marvellously supported; though I assure thee, I grow an old man, and feel infirmities of age marvellously stealing upon me.

Would my corruptions did as fast decrease. Pray on my behalf in the latter respect. The particulars of our late success Harry Vane or Gil. Pickering will impart to thee.

My love to all dear friends.

I rest thine,

Oliver Cromwell

Oliver Cromwell (1599-1658)
Dunbar, 4 September, 1650

Nothing could have given me greater pleasure that to get news of you. The prospect of remaining two months without hearing about you had been extremely disagreeable to me: that is to say, your little note was more than welcome.

I hope you are laying up a stock of good air and that you will come back to us in October. As for me, I think I shall not go anywhere; I shall stay in the country, where I spend the whole day in front of my open window or in the garden.

We have promised each other -- haven't we? -- to be at least great friends. If you will only not change your mind! For there are no promises that are binding; such things cannot be ordered at will. It would be a fine thing, just the same, in which I hardly dare believe, to pass our lives near each other, hypnotized by our dreams: your patriotic dream, our humanitarian dream, and our scientific dream.

Of all those dreams the last is, I believe, the only legitimate one. I mean by that that we are powerless to change the social order and, even if we were not, we should not know what to do; in taking action, no matter in what direction, we should never be sure of not doing more harm than good, by retarding some inevitable evolution.

From the scientific point of view, on the contrary, we may hope to do something; the ground is solider here, and any discovery that we may make, however small, will remain acquired knowledge.

See how it works out: it is agreed that we shall be great friends, but if you leave France in a year it would be an altogether too Platonic friendship, that of two creatures who would never see each other again. Wouldn't it be better for you to stay with me?

I know that this question angers you, and that you don't want to speak of it again -- and then, too, I feel so thoroughly unworthy of you from every point of view.

I thought of asking your permission to meet you by chance in Fribourg. But you are staying there, unless I am mistaken, only one day, and on that day you will of course belong to our friends the Kovalskis.

Believe me your very devoted
Pierre Curie

Pierre Curie (1859-1906)
August 10, 1894

But let me have this letter, containing nothing but your love; and tell me that you give me your lips, your hair, all that face that I have possessed, and tell me that we embrace - you and I!

O God, O God, when I think of it, my throat closes, my sight is troubled; my knees fail, ah, it is horrible to die, it is also horrible to love like this! What longing, what longing I have for you!

I beg you to let me have the letter I ask. I am dying.

Farewell.

Alfred de Musset
September 1, 1834

Sweetheart,

Please, please don't be so depressed. We'll be married soon, and then these lonesome nights will be over forever - and until we are, I am loving, loving every tiny minute of the day and night.

Maybe you won't understand this, but sometimes when I miss you most, it's hardest to write - and you always know when I make myself. Just the ache of it all - and I can't tell you.

If we were together, you'd feel how strong it is - you're so sweet when you're melancholy. I love your sad tenderness - when I've hurt you.

That's one of the reasons I could never be sorry for our quarrels - and they bothered you so. Those dear, dear little fusses, when I always tried so hard to make you kiss and forget - Scott - there's nothing in all the world I want but you - and your precious love.

All the material things are nothing. I'd just hate to live a sordid, colorless existence - because you'd soon love me less - and less - and I'd do anything - anything - to keep your heart for my own. I don't want to live - I want to love first, and live incidentally.

Why don't you feel that I'm waiting - I'll come to you, Lover, when you're ready. Don't don't ever think of the things you can't give me. You've trusted me with the dearest heart of all - and it's so damn much more than anybody else in all the world has ever had.

How can you think deliberately of life without me. If you should die - O Darling - darling Scott - It'd be like going blind. I know I would, too, I'd have no purpose in life - just a pretty decoration. Don't you think I was made for you? I feel like you had me ordered - and I was delivered to you - to be worn.

I want you to wear me, like a watch - charm or a button hole boquet - to the world. And then, when we're alone, I want to help - to know that you can't do anything without me.

I'm glad you wrote Mamma. It was such a nice sincere letter - and mine to St. Paul was very evasive and rambling. I've never, in all my life, been able to say anything to people older than me. Somehow I just instinctively avoid personal things with them - even my family. Kids are so much nicer.

F. Scott Fitzgerald (1896-1940)
Spring 1919

I will cover you with love when next I see you, with caresses, with ecstasy. I want to gorge yu with all the joys of the flesh, so that you faint and die. I want you to be amazed by me, and to confess to yourself that you had never even dreamed of such transports...

When you are old, I want you to recall those few hours, I want your dry bones to quiver with joy when you think of them.

Gustave Flaubert
August 15, 1846

Have you really not noticed, then, that here of all places, in this private, personal solitude that surrounds me, I have turned to you?

All the memories of my youth speak to me as I walk, just as the sea shells crunch under my feet on the beach. The crash of every wave awakens far-distant reverberations within me.

I hear the rumble of bygone days, and in my mind the whole endless series of old passions surges forward like the billows. I remember my spasms, my sorrows, gusts of desire that whistled like wind in the rigging, and vast vague longings that swirled in the dark like a flock of wild gulls in a storm cloud.

On whom should I lean, if not on you?

My weary mind turns for refreshment to the thought of you as a dusty traveler might sink onto a soft and grassy bank.

Gustave Flaubert
August 21, 1853

My letters will have shown you how lovely I am. I don't dine at Court, I see few people, and take my walks alone, and at every beautiful spot I wish you were there.

I can't help loving you more than is good for me; I shall feel all the happier when I see you again. I am always conscious of my nearness to you, your presence never leaves me. In you I have a measure for every woman, for everyone; in your love a measure for all that is to be.

Not in the sense that the rest of the world seems obscure tome, on the contrary, your love makes it clear; I see quite clearly what men are like and what they plan, wish, do and enjoy; I don't grudge them what they have, and comparing is a secret joy to me, possessing as I do such an imperishable treasure.

You in your household must feel as I often do in my affairs; we often don't notice objects simply because we don't choose to look at them, but things acquire an interest as soon as we see clearly the way they are related to each other.

For we always like to join in, and the good man takes pleasure in arranging, putting in order and furthering the right and its peaceful rule. Adieu, you whom I love a thousand times.

Johann Wolfgang von Goethe (1749-1832)

June 17, 1784

...and now, love, you with the warm heart and loving eyes, whose picture I kissed last night and whose lips I so often kiss in my dreams, whose love enriches me so bountifully with all pleasant memories and sweet anticipations, whose encircling arms shield me from so much evil and harm, whose caresses are so dear and so longed for awake and in slumber, making my heart beat faster, my flesh tremble and my brain giddy with delight, - whose feet I kiss and whose knees I embrace as a devotee kisses and embraces those of his idol, - my darling whose home is in my arms and whose resting place my bosom, who first came to them as a frightened bird but now loves to linger there till long after the midnight chimes have uttered their warning, - my life, with your generous soul, my heart's keeper and my true lover, - Good night: a good night and a fair one to thy sleeping eyes and wearied limb, the precursor of many bright, beautiful mornings when my kisses shall waken thee and my love shall greet thee.

Lyman

Lyman Hodge
February 10, 1867

Sophie,

To be with the people one loves, says La Bruyere is enough - to dream you are speaking to them, not speaking to them, thinking of them, thinking of the most indifferent things, but by their side, nothing else matters. O mon amie, how true that is! and it is also true that when one acquires such a habit, it becomes a necessary part of one's existence.

Alas! I well know, I should know too well, since the three months that I sigh, far away from thee, that I possess thee no more, than my happiness has departed. However, when every morning I wake up, I look for you, it seems to me that half of myself is missing, and that is too true.

Twenty times during the day, I ask myself where you are; judge how strong the illusion is, and how cruel it is to see it vanish. When I go to bed, I do not fail to make room for you; I push myself quite close to the wall and leave a great empty space in my small bed.

This movement is mechanical, these thoughts are involuntary. Ah! how one accustoms oneself to happiness.

Alas! one only knows it well when one has lost it, and I'm sure we have only learnt to appreciate how necessary we are to each other, since the thunderbolt has parted us. The source of our tears has not dried up, dear Sophie; we cannot become healed; we have enough in our hearts to love always, and, because of that, enough to weep always.

Gabriel

Count Gabriel Honore de Mirbeau

c 1780

To Adele Foucher

My dearest,

When two souls, which have sought each other for, however long in the throng, have finally found each other... a union, fiery and pure as they themselves are... begins on earth and continues forever in heaven.

This union is love, true love, a religion, which deifies the loved one, whose life comes from devotion and passion, and for which the greatest sacrifices are the sweetest delights.

This is the love which you inspire in me... Your soul is made to love with the purity and passion of angels; but perhaps it can only love another angel, in which case I must tremble with apprehension.

Yours forever,
Victor Hugo

Victor Hugo
1821

Friday evening, March 15, 1822.

After the two delightful evenings spent yesterday and the day before, I shall certainly not go out tonight, but will sit here at home and write to you. Besides, my Adele, my adorable and adored Adele, what have I not to tell you?

O, God! for two days, I have been asking myself every moment if such happiness is not a dream. It seems to me that what I feel is not of earth. I cannot yet comprehend this cloudless heaven.

You do not yet know, Adele, to what I had resigned myself. Alas, do I know it myself? Because I was weak, I fancied I was calm; because I was preparing myself for all the mad follies of despair, I thought I was courageous and resigned. Ah! let me cast myself humbly at your feet, you who are so grand, so tender and strong! I had been thinking that the utmost limit of my devotion could only be the sacrifice of my life; but you, my generous love, were ready to sacrifice for me the repose of yours.

...You have been privileged to receive every gift from nature, you have both fortitude and tears. Oh, Adele, do not mistake these words for blind enthusiasm - enthusiasm for you has lasted all my life, and increased day by day.

My whole soul is yours. If my entire existence had not been yours, the harmony of my being would have been lost, and I must have died - died inevitably.

These were my meditations, Adele, when the letter that was to bring me hope of else despair arrived. If you love me, you know what must have been my joy. What I know you may have felt, I will not describe.

Victor Hugo

1821

My Adele, why is there no word for this but joy? Is it because there is no power in human speech to express such happiness?

The sudden bound from mournful resignation to infinite felicity seemed to upset me. Even now I am still beside myself and sometimes I tremble lest I should suddenly awaken from this dream divine.

Oh, now you are mine! At last you are mine! Soon - in a few months, perhaps, my angel will sleep in my arms, will awaken in my arms, will live there.

All your thoughts at all moments, all your looks will be for me; all my thoughts, all my moments, all my looks, will be for you! My Adele!

Adieu, my angel, my beloved Adele! Adieu! I will kiss your hair and go to bed. Still I am far from you, but I can dream of you. Soon perhaps you will be at my side. Adieu; pardon the delirium of your husband who embraces you, and who adores you, both for this life and another.

Victor Hugo
March 15, 1822

You have been wonderful, my Juliette, all through these dark and violent days. If I needed love, you brought it to me, bless you! When, in my hiding places, always dangerous, after a night of waiting, I heard the key of my door trembling in your fingers, peril and darkness were no longer round me--what entered then was light!

We must never forget those terrible, but so sweet, hours when you were close to me in the intervals of fighting. Let us remember all our lives that dark little room, the ancient hangings, the two armchairs, side by side, the meal we ate off the corner of the table, the cold chicken you had brought; our sweet converse, your caresses, your anxieties, your devotion. You were surprised to find me calm and serene. Do you know whence came both calmness and serenity? From you...

Victor Hugo
December 31, 1851

My dear Nora,

It has just struck me. I came in at half past eleven. Since then I have been sitting in an easy chair like a fool. I could do nothing. I hear nothing but your voice. I am like a fool hearing you call me 'Dear.' I offended two men today by leaving them coolly. I wanted to hear your voice, not theirs. When I am with you I leave aside my contemptuous, suspicious nature.

I wish I felt your head on my shoulder. I think I will go to bed. I have been a half-hour writing this thing. Will you write something to me? I hope you will. How am I to sign myself? I won't sign anything at all, because I don't know what to sign myself.

James Joyce (1882-1941)

15 August, 1904

Fräulein Felice!

I am now going to ask you a favor which sounds quite crazy, and which I should regard as such, were I the one to receive the letter. It is also the very greatest test that even the kindest person could be put to.

Well, this is it: Write to me only once a week, so that your letter arrives on Sunday - for I cannot endure your daily letters, I am incapable of enduring them.

For instance, I answer one of your letters, then lie in bed in apparent calm, but my heart beats through my entire body and is conscious only of you. I belong to you; there is really no other way of expressing it, and that is not strong enough. But for this very reason I don't want to know what you are wearing; it confuses me so much that I cannot deal with life; and that's why I don't want to know that you are fond of me. If I did, how could I, fool that I am, go on sitting in my office, or here at home, instead of leaping onto a train with my eyes shut and opening them only when I am with you? Oh, there is a sad, sad reason for not doing so.

To make it short: My health is only just good enough for myself alone, not good enough for marriage, let alone fatherhood. Yet when I read your letter, I feel I could overlook even what cannot possibly be overlooked.

If only I had your answer now! And how horribly I torment you, and how I compel you, in the stillness of your room, to read this letter, as nasty a letter as has ever lain on your desk! Honestly, it strikes me sometimes that I prey like a spectre on your felicitous name! If only I had mailed Saturday's letter, in which I implored you never to write to me again, and in which I gave a similar promise.

Oh God, what prevented me from sending that letter? All would be well.

But is a peaceful solution possible now? Would it help if we wrote to each other only once a week? No, if my suffering could be cured by such means it would not be serious.

And already I foresee that I shan't be able to endure even the Sunday letters.

And so, to compensate for Saturday's lost opportunity, I ask you with what energy remains to me at the end of this letter: If we value our lives, let us abandon it all.

Did I think of signing myself Dein? No, nothing could be more false. No, I am forever fettered to myself, that's what I am, and that's what I must try to live with.

Franz Kafka (1883-1924)
11 November, 1912

Sweetest Fanny,

You fear, sometimes, I do not love you so much as you wish? My dear Girl I love you ever and ever and without re-serve. The more I have known you the more have I lov'd. In every way - even my jealousies have been agonies of Love, in the hottest fit I ever had I would have died for you. I have vex'd you too much. But for Love! Can I help it?

You are always new. The last of your kisses was ever the sweetest; the last smile the brightest; the last movement the gracefullest. When you pass'd my window home yester-day, I was fill'd with as much admiration as if I had then seen you for the first time. You uttered a half complaint once that I only lov'd your Beauty.

Have I nothing else then to love in you but that? Do not I see a heart naturally furnish'd with wings imprison itself with me?

No ill prospect has been able to turn your thoughts a mo-ment from me. This perhaps should be as much a subject of sorrow as joy - but I will not talk of that.

Even if you did not love me I could not help an entire devotion to you: how much more deeply then must I feel for you knowing you love me. My Mind has been the most discontented and restless one that ever was put into a body too small for it.

I never felt my Mind repose upon anything with complete and undistracted enjoyment - upon no person but you. When you are in the room my thoughts never fly out of window: you always concentrate my whole senses. The anxiety shown about our Love in your last note is an immense pleasure to me; however you must not suffer such speculations to molest you any more: not will I any more believe you can have the least pique against me. Brown is gone out - but here is Mrs Wylie - when she is gone I shall be awake for you. Remembrances to your Mother.

Your affectionate,
J. Keats

John Keats (1795-1821)
March 1820

To Fanny Brawne:

I cannot exist without you - I am forgetful of every thing but seeing you again - my life seems to stop there - I see no further. You have absorb'd me.

I have a sensation at the present moment as though I were dissolving...

I have been astonished that men could die martyrs for religion.

I have shudder'd at it - I shudder no more.

I could be martyr'd for my religion - love is my religion - I could die for that - I could die for you.

My creed is love and you are its only tenet - you have ravish'd me away by a power I cannot resist.

John Keats

John Keats (1795-1821)
March 1820

Wednesday Morning
[Kentish Town, 1820]

My Dearest Girl,

I have been a walk this morning with a book in my hand, but as usual I have been occupied with nothing but you: I wish I could say in an agreeable manner.

I am tormented day and night. They talk of my going to Italy. 'Tis certain I shall never recover if I am to be so long separate from you: yet with all this devotion to you I cannot persuade myself into

any confidence of you...

You are to me an object intensely desirable - the air I breathe in a room empty of you in unhealthy.

I am not the same to you - no - you can wait - you have a thousand activities - you can be happy without me. Any party, anything to fill up the day has been enough.

How have you pass'd this month? Who have you smil'd with? All this may seem savage in me.

You do no feel as I do - you do not know what it is to love - one day you may - your time is not come...

I cannot live without you, and not only you but chaste you; virtuous you. The Sun rises and sets, the day passes, and you follow the bent of your inclination to a certain extent - you have no conception of the quantity of miserable feeling that passes through me in a day. Be serious! Love is not a plaything - and again do not write unless you can do it with a crystal conscience.

I would sooner die for want of you than.

Yours for ever
J. Keats

John Keats (1795-1821)
1820

I have waited patiently for one whole day without news of you; I have been counting the time and that's what it must be. But a second day - I can see no reason for it, unless my servants have grown lazy or been captured by the enemy, for I dare not put the blame on you, my beautiful angel: I am too confident of your affection - which is certainly due to me, for my love was never greater, nor my desire more urgent; that is why I repeat this refrain in all my letters: come, come, come, my dear love.

Honor with your presence the man who, if only he were free, would go a thousand miles to throw himself at your feet and never move from there. As for what is happening here, we have drained the water from the moat, but our cannons are not going to be in place until Friday when, God willing, I will dine in town.

The day after you reach Mantes, my sister will arrive at Anet, where I will have the pleasure of seeing you every day.

I am sending you a bouquet of orange blossom that I have just received. I kiss the hands of the Vicomtess [Gabrielle's sister, Fran oise] if she is there, and of my good friend [his sister, Catherine of Bourbon], and as for you, my dear love, I kiss your feet a million times.

Henry IV of France (1553-1610)

June 16, 1593

To Anne Boleyn

My Mistress and Friend,

I and my heart put ourselves in your hands, begging you to recommend us to your good grace and not to let absence lessen your affection... or myself the pang of absence is already to great, and when I think of the increase of what I must needs suffer it would be well nigh intolerable but for my firm hope of your unchangeable affection...

Henry VIII (1491-1547)

1528

In debating with myself the contents of your letters I have been put to a great agony; not knowing how to understand them, whether to my disadvantage as shown in some places, or to my advantage as in others. I beseech you now with all my heart definitely to let me know your whole mind as to the love between us; for necessity compels me to plague you for a reply, having been for more than a year now struck by the dart of love, and being uncertain either of failure or of finding a place in your heart and affection, which point has certainly kept me for some time from naming you my mistress, since if you only love me with an ordinary love the name is not appropriate to you, seeing that it stands for an uncommon position very remote from the ordinary; but if it pleases you to do the duty of a true, loyal mistress and friend, and to give yourself body and heart to me, who have been, and will be, your very loyal servant (if your rigour does not forbid me), I promise you that not only the name will be due to you, but also to take you as my sole mistress, casting off all others than yourself out of mind and affection, and to serve you only; begging you to make me a complete reply to this my rude letter as to how far and in what I can trust; and if it does not please you to reply in writing, to let me know of some place where I can have it by word of mouth, the which place I will seek out with all my heart. No more for fear of wearying you. Written by the hand of him who would willingly remain yours.

HR

Henry VIII (1491-1547)
1528

Thursday morning, 1834

My heart overflows with emotion and joy! I do not know what heavenly languor, what infinite pleasure permeates it and burns me up. It is as if I had never loved!!! Tell me whence these uncanny disturbances spring, these inexpressible foretastes of delight, these divine, tremors of love.

Oh! all this can only spring from you, sister, angel, woman, Marie! All this can only be, is surely nothing less than a gentle ray streaming from your fiery soul, or else some secret poignant teardrop which you have long since left in my breast.

My God, my God, never force us apart, take pity on us! But what am I saying? Forgive my weakness, how couldst Thou divide us! Thou wouldst have nothing but pity for us... No no! It is not in vain that our flesh and our souls quicken and become immortal through Thy Word, which cries out deep within us Father, Father...out Thy hand to us, that our broken hearts seek their refuge in Thee...O! we thank, bless and praise Thee, O God, for all that Thou has given us, and all that Thou hast prepared for us....

This is to be -- to be! Marie! Marie!

Oh let me repeat that name a hundred times, a thousand times over; for three days now it has lived within me, oppressed me, set me afire. I am not writing to you, no, I am close beside you. I see you, I hear you. Eternity in your arms... Heaven, Hell, everything, all is within you, redoubled... Oh! Leave me free to rave in my delirium.

Drab, tame, constricting reality is no longer enough for me. We must live our lives to the full, loving and suffering to extremes!

Franz

Franz Liszt (1811-1886)
1834

December 1834

Marie! Marie!

Oh let me repeat that name a hundred times, a thousand times over;

for three days now it has lived within me, oppressed me, set me afire.

I am not writing to you, no, I am close beside you.

I see you, I hear you... Eternity in your arms...

Heaven, hell, all is within you and even more than all...

Oh! Leave me free to rave in my delirium.

Mean, cautious, narrow reality is no longer enough for me.

We must live out lives to the full, our loves, our sorrow...!

Oh! you believe me capable of self-sacrifice, chastity, temperance and piety, do you not?

But let no more be said of this... it is for you to question, to draw conclusions, to save me as you see fit.

Let me be mad, senseless since you can do nothing, nothing at all for me.

It is good for me to speak to you now.

This is to be! To be!

Franz Liszt (1811-1886)

1834

Oakland, April 3, 1901

Dear Anna:

Did I say that the human might be filed in categories? Well, and if I did, let me qualify - not all humans. You elude me. I cannot place you, cannot grasp you. I may boast that of nine out of ten, under given circumstances, I can forecast their action; that of nine out of ten, by their word or action, I may feel the pulse of their hearts. But of the tenth I despair. It is beyond me. You are that tenth.

Were ever two souls, with dumb lips, more incongruously matched! We may feel in common - surely, we oftimes do - and when we do not feel in common, yet do we understand; and yet we have no common tongue.

Spoken words do not come to us. We are unintelligible. God must laugh at the mummery.

The one gleam of sanity through it all is that we are both large temperamentally, large enough to often understand.

True, we often understand but in vague glimmering ways, by dim perceptions, like ghosts, which, while we doubt, haunt us with their truth. And still, I, for one, dare not believe; for you are that tenth which I may not forecast.

Am I unintelligible now? I do not know. I imagine so. I cannot find the common tongue.

Large temperamentally - that is it. It is the one thing that brings us at all in touch. We have, flashed through us, you and I, each a bit of universal, and so we draw together. And yet we are so different.

I smile at you when you grow enthusiastic? It is a forgivable smile - nay, almost an envious smile. I have lived twenty-five years of repression. I learned not to be enthusiastic. It is a hard lesson to forget.

I begin to forget, but it is so little. At the best, before I die, I cannot hope to forget all or most. I can exult, now that I am learning, in little things, in other things; but of my things, and secret things doubly mine, I cannot, I cannot.

Do I make myself intelligible? Do you hear my voice? I fear not. There are poseurs. I am the most successful of them all.

Jack

Jack London (1876-1916)
April 3, 1901

Mainz October 17, 1790

PS. While I was writing the last page, tear after tear fell on the paper. But I must cheer up - catch! An astonishing number of kisses are flying about - The deuce! - I see a whole crowd of them! Ha! Ha!

I have just caught three - They are delicious! You can still answer this letter, but you must address your reply to Linz, Poste Restante. That is the safest course. As I do not yet know for certain whether I shall go to Regensburg, I can't tell you anything definite. Just write on the cover that the letter is to be kept until called for.

Adieu - Dearest, most beloved little wife - Take care of your health - and don't think of walking into town. Do write and tell me how you like our new quarters - Adieu.

I kiss you millions of times.

Wolfgang Amadeus Mozart (1756-1791)
October 17, 1790

Could I see you without passion, or be absent from you without pain, I need not beg your pardon for thus renewing my vows that I love you more than health, or any happiness here or hereafter.

Everything you do is a new charm to me, and though I have lanquished for seven long tedious years of desire, jealously despairing, yet every minute I see you I still discover something new and more bewitching.

Consider how I love you; what would I not renounce or enterprise for you? I much have you mine, or I am miserable, and nothing but knowing which shall be the happy hour can make the rest of my years that are to come tolerable. Give me a word or two of comfort, or resolve never to look on me more, for I cannot bear a kind look and after it a cruel denial.

This minute my heart aches for you; and, if I cannot have a right in yours, I wish it would ache till I could complain to you no longer.

Thomas Otway

1678

My Darling Josephine:

Am nearly through with my writing. Am brain weary with the thousand and one imperative details and things to think of. Everything thus far has gone well, too well I am afraid, and I am (solely on general principles) somewhat suspicious of the future. The ship is in better shape than before; the party and crew are apparently harmonious; I have 21 Eskimo men (against 23 last time) but the total of men women and children is only 50 as against 67 before owing to a more careful selection as to children... I have landed supplies here, and leave two men ostensibly on behalf of Cook.

As a matter of fact I have established here the sub-base which last I established at Victoria Head, as a precaution in event of loss of the Roosevelt either going up this fall or coming down next summer. In some respects this is an advantage as on leaving here there is nothing to delay me or keep me from taking either side of the Channel going up, the conditions give me entire control of the situation...

You have been with me constantly, sweetheart. At Kangerdlooksoah I looked repeatedly at Ptarmigan Island and thought of the time we camped there. At Nuuatoksoah I landed where we were. And on the 11th we passed the mouth of Bowdoin Bay in brilliant weather, and as long as I could I kept my eyes on Anniversary Lodge. We have been great chums dear. Tell Marie to remember what I told her, tell "Mister Man" [Robert Peary, Jr.] to remember "straight and strong and clean and honest", obey orders, and never forget that Daddy put "Mut" in his charge till he himself comes back to take her. In fancy I kiss your dear eyes and lips and cheeks sweetheart; and dream of you and my children, and my home till I come again. Kiss my babies for me.

Aufwiedersehen.
Love, Love, Love.
Your Bert

P.S. August 18, 9 a.m ... Tell Marie that her fir pillow perfumes me to sleep.

Robert Peary (1856-1920)
August 17, 1908

You shall now receive (my dear wife) my last words in these my last lines. My love I send you that you may keep it when I am dead, and my counsel that you may remember it when I am no more.

I would not by my will present you with sorrows (dear Besse) let them go to the grave with me and be buried in the dust. And seeing that it is not God's will that I should see you any more in this life, bear it patiently, and with a heart like thy self.

First, I send you all the thanks which my heart can conceive, or my words can rehearse for your many travails, and care taken for me, which though they have not taken effect as you wished, yet my debt to you is not the less; but pay it I never shall in this world.

Secondly, I beseech you for the love you bear me living, do not hide your self many days, but by your travails seek to help your miserable fortunes and the right of your poor child. Thy mourning cannot avail me, I am but dust...

Remember your poor child for his father's sake, who chose you, and loved you in his happiest times.

Get those letters which I wrote to the Lords, wherein I sued for my life; God is my witness it was for you and yours that I desired life, but it is true that I disdained my self for begging of it: for know it that your son is the son of a true man, and one who in his own respect despiseth death and all his misshapen and ugly forms.

I cannot write much, God he knows how hardly I steal this time while others sleep, and it is also time that I should separate my thoughts from the world. Beg my dead body which living was denied thee; and either lay it at Sherburne or in Exeter Church, by my Father and Mother; I can say no more, time and death call me away....

Written with the dying hand of sometimes they Husband, but now alas overthrown. Yours that was, but now not my own.

Walter Raleigh

Sir Walter Raleigh (1552-1618)

1603

Dearest Bunny,

Do you know what this is - a wedding anniversary letter. I think it should arrive about on the right date. Do you remember that hot June day thirty-three years ago? The church jammed - Father with a lovely waistcoat with small blue spots--the Rough Riders - the ushers in cutaways - the crowds in the street - your long white veil and tight little bodice - the reception at Aunt Harriet's - Uncle Ed - your mother with one of her extraordinary hats that stood straight up.

And do you remember what the world was then - little and cozy - a different order of things, wars considered on the basis of a Dick [Richard Harding] Davis novel, a sort of "As it was in the beginning" atmosphere over life. We've come a long way down a strange road since then.

Nothing has happened as we imagined it would except our children. We never thought we'd roam the world. We never thought our occupations and interests would cover such a range.

We never thought that our thirty-third anniversary would find us deep in our second war and me again at the front. Well, darling, we've lived up to the most important part of the ceremony, "In sickness and in health, for richer for poorer, till death do you part."

Much, much love.

Theodore Roosevelt, Jr. (1887-1944)

May 20, 1943

I don't know anything dreadful enough to liken to you - you are like a sweet forest of pleasant glades and whispering branches - where people wander on and on in its playing shadows they know not how far - and when they come near the centre of it, it is all cold and impenetrable - and when they would fain turn, lo - they are hedged with briars and thorns and cannot escape...

You are like the bright - soft - swelling - lovely fields of a high glacier covered with fresh morning snow - which is heavenly to the eye - and soft and winning on the foot - but beneath, there are winding clefts and dark places in its cold - cold ice - where men fall, and rise not again.

John Ruskin
December 1847

Clara,

How happy your last letters have made me - those since Christmas Eve! I should like to call you by all the endearing epithets, and yet I can find no lovelier word than the simple word 'dear,' but there is a particular way of saying it. My dear one, then, I have wept for joy to think that you are mine, and often wonder if I deserve you.

One would think that no one man's heart and brain could stand all the things that are crowded into one day. Where do these thousands of thoughts, wishes, sorrows, joys and hopes come from? Day in, day out, the procession goes on. But how light-hearted I was yesterday and the day before! There shone out of your letters so noble a spirit, such faith, such a wealth of love!

What would I not do for love of you, my own Clara! The knights of old were better off; they could go through fire or slay dragons to win their ladies, but we of today have to content ourselves with more prosaic methods, such as smoking fewer cigars, and the like. After all, though, we can love, knights or no knights; and so, as ever, only the times change, not men's hearts...

You cannot think how your letter has raised and strengthened me... You are splendid, and I have much more reason to be proud of you than you of me. I have made up my mind, though, to read all your wishes in your face. Then you will think, even though you don't say it, that your Robert is a really good sort, that he is entirely yours, and he loves you more than words can say.

You shall indeed have cause to think so in the happy future. I still see you as you looked in your little cap that last evening. I still hear you call me du. Clara, I heard nothing of what you said but that du. Don't you remember?

But I see you in many another unforgettable guise. Once you were in a black dress, going to the theatre with Emilia List; it was during our separation. I know you will not have forgotten; it is vivid with me. Another time you were walking in the Thomasgasschen with an umbrella up, and you avoided me in desperation. And yet another time, as you were putting on your hat after a concert, our eyes happened to meet, and yours were full of the old unchanging love.

I picture you in all sorts of ways, as I have seen you since.

I did not look at you much, but you charmed me so immeasurably... Ah, I can never praise you enough for yourself or for your love of me, which I don't really deserve.

Robert

Robert Schumann

1838

To 'Stella' Beatrice Campbell

I want my rapscallionly fellow vagabond.

I want my dark lady. I want my angel -

I want my tempter.

I want my Freia with her apples.

I want the lighter of my seven lamps of beauty, honour,

laughter, music, love, life and immortality...

I want my inspiration, my folly, my happiness,

my divinity, my madness, my selfishness,

my final sanity and sanctification,

my transfiguration, my purification,

my light across the sea,

my palm across the desert,

my garden of lovely flowers,

my million nameless joys,

my day's wage,

my night's dream,

my darling and

my star...

George Bernard Shaw
February 27, 1913

Smith-street, West-minster

Madam,

I lay down last night with your image in my thoughts, and have awak'd this morning in the same contemplation. The pleasing transport ith which I'me delighted, has a sweet-nesse in it attended with a train of ten thousand soft desires, anxieties, and cares.

The day arises on my hopes with new brightnesse; youth beauty and innocence are the charming objects that steal me from myself, and give me joys above the reach of ambition pride or glory. Believe me, Fair One, to throw myself at yr feet is giving myself the highest blisse I know of earth.

Oh hasten ye minutes! Bring on the happy morning wherein to be ever her's will make me look down on Thrones!

Dear Molly I am tenderly, passionately, faithfully thine,
Richard Steele

Richard Steele

1707

I have something stupid and ridiculous to tell you. I am foolishly writing to you instead of having told you this, I do not know why, when returning from that walk.

Tonight I shall be annoyed at having done so. You will laugh in my face, will take me for a maker of phrases in all my relations with you hitherto. You will show me the door and you will think I am lying.

I am in love with you. I have been thus since the first day I called on you.

Alfred de Musset

1833

Cat: my cat: If only you would write to me: My love, oh Cat. This is not, as it seems from the address above, a dive, a joint, saloon, etc. but the honourable & dignified headquarters of the dons of the University of Chicago.

I love you. That is all I know. But all I know, too, is that I am writing into space: the kind of dreadful, unknown space I am just going to enter. I am going to Iowa, Illinois, Idaho, Indindiana, but these, though mis-spelt, are on the map. You are not.

Have you forgotten me? I am the man you used to say you loved. I used to sleep in your arms - do you remember? But you never write.

You are perhaps mindless of me. I am not of you. I love you.

There isn't a moment of any hideous day when I do not say to myself. 'It will be alright. I shall go home. Caitlin loves me. I love Caitlin.'

But perhaps you have forgotten. If you have forgotten, or lost your affection for me, please, my Cat, let me know. I Love You.

Dylan

Dylan Thomas
March 16, 1950

I already love in you your beauty, but I am only beginning to love in you that which is eternal and ever precious - your heart, your soul. Beauty one could get to know and fall in love with in one hour and cease to love it as speedily; but the soul one must learn to know. Believe me, nothing on earth is given without labour, even love, the most beautiful and natural of feelings.

Count Leo Tolstoy
November 2, 1856

Life has become very dear to me, and I am very glad that I love. My life and my love are one. "But you are faced with a 'no, never never'" is your reply. My answer to that is, "Old boy, for the present I look upon that 'no, never never' as a block of ice which I press to my heart to thaw." Vincent Van Gogh, famous French artist to Theo, his brother, describing his passion for his cousin, Kee. She never withdrew from her position of 'no, never never'.

Vincent Van Gogh
September 7, 1881

I am a prisoner here in the name of the King; they can take my life, but not the love that I feel for you. Yes, my adorable mistress, to-night I shall see you, and if I had to put my head on the block to do it.

For heaven's sake, do not speak to me in such disastrous terms as you write; you must live and be cautious; beware of madame your mother as of your worst enemy. What do I say? Beware of everybody; trust no one; keep yourself in readiness, as soon as the moon is visible; I shall leave the hotel incognito, take a carriage or a chaise, we shall drive like the wind to Sheveningen; I shall take paper and ink with me; we shall write our letters.

If you love me, reassure yourself; and call all your strength and presence of mind to your aid; do not let your mother notice anything, try to have your pictures, and be assured that the menace of the greatest tortures will not prevent me to serve you. No, nothing has the power to part me from you; our love is based upon virtue, and will last as long as our lives.

Adieu, there is nothing that I will not brave for your sake;
you deserve much more than that. Adieu, my dear heart!

Arout
(Voltaire)

Voltaire (1694-1778)

The Hague 1713

My golden child, my pearl, my precious stone, my crown, my queen and empress. You dear darling of my heart, my highest and most precious, my all and everything, my wife, the baptism of my children, my tragic play, my posthumous reputation. Ach! You are my second better self, my virtues, my merits, my hope, the forgiveness of my sins, my future sanctity, O little daughter of heaven, my child of God, my intercessor, my guardian angel, my cherubim and seraph, how I love you!

Henry von Kleist

1810

The White House

September 19, 1915

My noble, incomparable Edith, I do not know how to express or analyze the conflicting emotions that have surged like a storm through my heart all night long. I only know that first and foremost in all my thoughts has been the glorious confirmation you gave me last night - without effort, unconsciously, as of course - of all I have ever thought of your mind and heart.

You have the greatest soul, the noblest nature, the sweetest, most loving heart I have ever known, and my love, my reverence, my admiration for you, you have increased in one evening as I should have thought only a lifetime of intimate, loving association could have increased them.

You are more wonderful and lovely in my eyes than you ever were before; and my pride and joy and gratitude that you should love me with such a perfect love are beyond all expression, except in some great poem which I cannot write.

Your own,
Woodrow

Woodrow Wilson
1915

You are suffering, my dearest creature - only now have I learned that letters must be posted very early in the morning on Mondays to Thursdays - the only days on which the mail-coach goes from here to K. - You are suffering - Ah, wherever I am, there you are also - I will arrange it with you and me that I can live with you. What a life!!! thus!!! without you - pursued by the goodness of mankind hither and thither - which I as little want to deserve as I deserve it - Humility of man towards man - it pains me - and when I consider myself in relation to the universe, what am I and what is He - whom we call the greatest - and yet - herein lies the divine in man - I weep when I reflect that you will probably not receive the first report from me until Saturday - Much as you love me - I love you more - But do not ever conceal yourself from me - good night - As I am taking the baths I must go to bed - Oh God - so near! so far! Is not our love truly a heavenly structure, and also as firm as the vault of heaven?

Ludwig van Beethoven (1770-1827)
July 6, 1806

Good morning, on July 7

Though still in bed, my thoughts go out to you, my Immortal Beloved, now and then joyfully, then sadly, waiting to learn whether or not fate will hear us - I can live only wholly with you or not at all - Yes, I am resolved to wander so long away from you until I can fly to your arms and say that I am really at home with you, and can send my soul enwrapped in you into the land of spirits - Yes, unhappily it must be so - You will be the more contained since you know my fidelity to you.

No one else can ever possess my heart - never - never - Oh God, why must one be parted from one whom one so loves. And yet my life in V is now a wretched life - Your love makes me at once the happiest and the unhappiest of men - At my age I need a steady, quiet life - can that be so in our connection?

My angel, I have just been told that the mailcoach goes every day - therefore I must close at once so that you may receive the letter at once - Be calm, only by a calm consideration of our existence can we achieve our purpose to live together - Be calm - love me - today - yesterday - what tearful longings for you - you - you - my life - my all - farewell. Oh continue to love me - never misjudge the most faithful heart of your beloved.

ever thine

ever mine

ever ours

Ludwig van Beethoven (1770-1827)

July 7, 1806

So in our connection? My angel, I have just been told that the mailcoach goes every day - therefore I must close at once so that you may receive the letter at once - Be calm, only by a calm consideration of our existence can we achieve our purpose to live together - Be calm - love me - today - yesterday - what tearful longings for you - you - you - my life - my all - farewell. Oh continue to love me - never misjudge the most faithful heart of your beloved.

ever thine

ever mine

ever ours

Ludwig van Beethoven (1770-1827)

July 7, 1806

ALSO AVAILABLE :

Love Letter of Great Men

Vol. 2

Made in the USA
Lexington, KY
13 November 2014